Original title:
Horizons Blooming with Dreams

Author: Johan Kirsipuu
ISBN HARDBACK: 978-9908-1-3085-9
ISBN PAPERBACK: 978-9908-1-3086-6
ISBN EBOOK: 978-9908-1-3087-3

Infinite Paths to Discover

Whispers call from distant lands,
Beneath the stars, where wonder stands.
Footsteps light on winding ways,
Embrace the night, the dawn of days.

Each trail unfolds with secrets old,
Stories of the brave and bold.
Through forests deep and mountains high,
Infinite paths beneath the sky.

The world abounds with hidden sights,
Magic blooms in soft twilight.
With every turn, a lesson waits,
In every heart, adventure states.

Echoes of laughter fill the air,
Journeys made with love and care.
A tapestry of dreams to weave,
In each new step, we dare believe.

The Color of Longing

Crimson skies of fading dusk,
A heart encased in gentle husk.
Within the shadows, whispers sigh,
Yearning notes like birds that fly.

Azure waves crash by the shore,
A melody of wanting more.
With every tear and every smile,
Longing stretches every mile.

Golden hues of memories bright,
In fleeting moments, hearts take flight.
A dance of dreams in twilight's glow,
Chasing echoes of long ago.

Emerald fields that beckon close,
In silence wrapped, the heart's morose.
Colors blend in soft embrace,
As longing finds its sacred place.

Serenades of a New Day

Morning breaks with tender light,
Birds aloft in joyful flight.
Songs of hope fill the air,
Awakening dreams everywhere.

Whispers of dawn, a soft refrain,
In the stillness, joy and pain.
Each sunbeam a promise made,
In the glow, our fears will fade.

Waves of gold dance on the sea,
Nature's rhythm, wild and free.
A symphony of life begins,
With every note, the spirit grins.

Gentle breeze through branches sways,
Nature's chorus sings our praise.
As shadows fade and bright times show,
In each heartbeat, love will grow.

Journeys Beyond the Mundane

A step away from time's embrace,
In every heartbeat, find our place.
Wander far from daily drudge,
Seek the magic, feel theudge.

Beyond the walls of comfort's sigh,
Adventure waits as dreams apply.
In hidden paths and winding turns,
The flame of wanderlust still burns.

Each moment counts, the clock unwinds,
With every breath, new treasure finds.
Let go of fear, seize the chance,
In every heartbeat lies a dance.

From city streets to mountain peaks,
The soul ignites, the spirit speaks.
Journeys vast, both near and far,
Beyond the mundane, wish on a star.

Butterflies in the Breeze

Delicate whispers on gentle winds,
Colors dance where the sunlight spins.
Moments flutter, fleeting and light,
Nature's palette, a glorious sight.

Petals sway in a fragrant embrace,
Whirling softly, they find their place.
Through gardens lush, a choreographed reel,
The magic of life, so vivid and real.

Children laugh, a joyous sound,
Chasing dreams on this vibrant ground.
Innocence twirls like the wings above,
A reminder of purity, hope, and love.

As daylight fades, their dance may cease,
But in our hearts, they grant us peace.
With every breeze, a new tale starts,
Whispers of joy to fill our hearts.

Lighthouses of the Soul

Stalwart towers on the rocky coast,
Guiding ships, they stand, a proud host.
Flickering beams in the night sky,
They chase the darkness, let courage fly.

In a tempest's rage, they brightly shine,
Holding the promise of safety divine.
With each wave crashing, the call persists,
A beacon of hope that always exists.

Within the heart, these lighthouses dwell,
Whispers of solace, the stories they tell.
Through life's rough seas and gentle tides,
They light the way where love abides.

Every flicker beckons the lost,
Teaching us strength, no matter the cost.
Anchored in faith, we look to the shore,
Guided by light, forevermore.

The Spirit of Exploration

Stars above, a shimmering guide,
Boundless paths where dreams reside.
Curiosity stirs the restless heart,
Adventure awaits, a brand new start.

Mountains tall and valleys deep,
Secrets of the world, ours to keep.
The journey calls with whispers sweet,
Embracing each moment, life's heartbeat.

Windswept shores and ancient trails,
Each step forward, where wonder prevails.
Chasing horizons beneath the skies,
In every heartbeat, the spirit flies.

Through forests thick and rivers wide,
The beauty of nature, our constant guide.
With open arms, we greet the new,
In the spirit of exploration, we pursue.

Unfolding in Technicolor

A canvas bright with vibrant hues,
Life unfolds in splendid views.
Every moment, a brushstroke bold,
Tales of the heart yearning to be told.

Dreamers dance in brilliant light,
Creating visions that take flight.
Colors blend in a swirling embrace,
Artistry blooms in a timeless space.

Threads of passion weave the night,
Painting shadows that shimmer bright.
In every glance, a story we find,
Unfolding layers of the heart and mind.

With each dawn, a fresh debut,
New adventures, a vibrant view.
Together we laugh, together we cry,
In technicolor dreams, we reach for the sky.

Unfolding Vistas Await

Beneath the azure sky,
Mountains rise in golden light,
Whispers of the gentle breeze,
Nature's beauty shines so bright.

Fields of green stretch far and wide,
Each flower blooms in soft embrace,
Rivers dance in joyous flow,
A world of magic, time and space.

Clouds drift softly overhead,
Casting shadows on the ground,
Hope unfurls with every step,
Adventure waits to be found.

Through valleys deep, we wander free,
With every turn, a sight divine,
Unfolding vistas call to me,
In nature's arms, our souls entwine.

So let us roam, hand in hand,
Together facing skies so blue,
With every heartbeat, we shall stand,
Exploring dreams that feel so true.

Memories Adrift on Breezes

Soft echoes of laughter rise,
Carried on the evening air,
Fragments of a time gone by,
Moments cherished, beyond compare.

The scent of pine and ocean salt,
Takes me back to days of yore,
Whispers stir the quiet night,
Reminding me what I adore.

Faded photographs, dusty frames,
Hold stories only I can tell,
Each glance a key to yesterday,
In memories, we find our spell.

Breezes tease with tales of love,
As shadows dance on moonlit lakes,
In dreams, the past comes alive,
Where every sigh and heartbeat wakes.

So let the winds guide my soul,
To shores where memories meet the sea,
For in those moments, I am whole,
Adrift, forever, wild and free.

Paths Beneath the Silver Moon

Guided by the silver light,
Nighttime whispers draw us near,
Through the trees, a winding path,
Where dreams and starlight intertwine.

Each step upon the quiet ground,
Nights serenade the world around,
With every heartbeat, time slows down,
As shadows dance and magic's found.

The moon, a guardian in the dark,
Illuminates our wandering quest,
Where secrets hide and wishes spark,
In the night's embrace, I feel blessed.

Among the stars, our spirits soar,
With silence, stories come alive,
Each trail leads to some distant shore,
In nocturnal bliss, we will thrive.

So let us walk this path of dreams,
Beneath a sky that feels so vast,
With every breath, our love redeems,
In gentle night, our hearts hold fast.

Spectrums of Forgotten Visions

Fractured glimmers of the past,
Like prisms shining in the night,
Colors swirl in memories cast,
Spectrums dance, a haunting sight.

Lost in thoughts, the shadows play,
Creating forms that fade and glide,
Unraveling tales in shades of gray,
Where hopes and fears so often bide.

In whispers soft, the stories lie,
Echoes of what once seemed real,
Each flicker an unspoken sigh,
With longing hearts, the truth we feel.

Yet in the darkness, light can bloom,
Painting dreams within the heart,
As spectrums weave through shadowed room,
In every tear, a brand new start.

So let us find those visions lost,
In each hue, a life revived,
For every path has its own cost,
In the colors, our souls survive.

Untamed Vistas

The mountains rise with pride,
Whispers of the wild inside.
Rivers carve their ancient tune,
Beneath the watchful silver moon.

Here the winds sing free and bold,
Stories of the earth retold.
Sunset paints the sky with fire,
Nature's breath, our hearts inspire.

Fields of green stretch far and wide,
In their beauty, dreams abide.
A canvas vast, we roam and seek,
In untamed vistas, spirit unique.

Creatures dance in shadowed glen,
Life is fierce, yet soft again.
Every step a gift revealed,
In this realm, our souls are healed.

Nature's pulse, a steady beat,
Echoes call, life feels complete.
Untamed vistas, wild and free,
A refuge for the heart to be.

Tapestries of Tomorrow's Vision

Threads of hope weave through the day,
Turning shadows into play.
Colors bright, they intertwine,
Charting paths where dreams align.

Every stitch a future cast,
In the loom, our hearts hold fast.
Whispers of the journey told,
In the fabric, bright and bold.

Patterns shift with every choice,
In the silence, hear the voice.
Tomorrow's vision clear and bright,
In the tapestry, we find light.

Time unfurls its careful hand,
Futures waiting, grandly planned.
Seek the dreams that draw you near,
In the fabric, lose all fear.

Tapestries of hope and grace,
Woven strong in this vast space.
A story yet to be unfurled,
In our hands, we shape the world.

Nightfall of Forgotten Dreams

When the sun bids soft adieu,
Whispers reign in shades of blue.
Stars emerge, a silver seam,
In the night, forgotten dream.

Time reveals what lies beneath,
Memories in silence wreathe.
Lost ambitions softly sigh,
Beneath the vast and open sky.

Shadows dance on moonlit ground,
Echoes of what could be found.
Once bright visions fade away,
In the night, they softly sway.

Yet within the dark's embrace,
Hope ignites with gentle grace.
In the quiet, seeds of light,
Revive the dreams lost from sight.

Nightfall brings a chance anew,
To awaken what's still true.
In the stillness, we believe,
From forgotten dreams, we weave.

The Dance of Ambitions

In a ballroom of the mind,
Dreams and hopes are intertwined.
Every heartbeat fuels the flame,
Ambitions rise, no one the same.

Twisting, turning, steps aligned,
With every turn, new paths we find.
Chasing visions, bright and clear,
In this dance, we shed all fear.

Rhythms of our eager hearts,
In the music, courage starts.
Every leap a chance to grow,
In the dance, our spirits flow.

Together we create the tune,
Underneath the watchful moon.
With each motion, dreams expand,
In this dance, we take a stand.

The stage is set, the lights aglow,
Ambitions surge, the world below.
In our steps, the future gleams,
In this dance, we chase our dreams.

Horizons Unseen

In twilight's hush, dreams unfold,
Veils of mystery, tales untold.
Stars whisper secrets in the night,
Guiding hearts to embrace the light.

The shore of hope, a distant call,
Waves of promise rise and fall.
With each glance, horizons await,
Inviting souls to dare their fate.

Beneath the sky, a canvas wide,
Colors blend where wonders reside.
Lunar beams dance on silver streams,
Painting paths of unspoken dreams.

Onward we trek, through shadows cast,
Chasing visions, shadows of the past.
Every step, a chance to soar,
Horizons seen, forevermore.

In the silence, courage blooms,
Breaking through the ancient tombs.
New beginnings, bright and free,
Horizons unseen, destiny.

A Symphony of Possibilities

Echoes of laughter, notes in the air,
Every heartbeat sings, a world laid bare.
Melodies swirl, inviting and free,
A symphony plays, calling to me.

Gentle whispers, soft as a breeze,
Dancing to rhythms among the trees.
Each note a promise, a chance to explore,
Awakening dreams, forevermore.

Unified voices, harmonies bright,
Together we rise, igniting the night.
Hand in hand, we'll weave our song,
In this grand dance, we all belong.

The future hums with potential and grace,
In every silence, a warm embrace.
With every moment, the music expands,
A symphony shared, in countless hands.

Through every dawn, let visions unfurl,
A symphony plays, embracing the world.
With hearts unbound, we'll reach for the skies,
In a chorus of wonders, forever we'll rise.

Fragments of Tomorrow's Applause

Shattered reflections, pieces align,
In disarray, a spark will shine.
Each fragment whispers, a story to tell,
A journey begun, where shadows dwell.

Moments entwined in the fabric of time,
Building a canvas, unique, sublime.
In every heartbeat, the echoes will play,
Fragments of tomorrow, brightening the day.

With every misstep, we learn to embrace,
The beauty of flaws within every space.
As dreams bloom gently, like flowers in spring,
From whispers of hope, brave voices will sing.

Applause for the past, the lessons we've learned,
In the dance of our lives, new fires are burned.
The future awaits, with open arms wide,
Fragments of tomorrow, the heart of our pride.

Together we rise, in harmony's grace,
Creating a rhythm in life's vast embrace.
Applause for the journey, the rise, and the fall,
In every heartbeat, a story for all.

Shadows Playing with Light

Dancing softly, shadows draw near,
Twisting and twirling, free of fear.
In candle's glow, a delicate lace,
Shadows playing, creating space.

Flickering whispers in twilight's embrace,
Merging with dawn, a gentle race.
Light and dark in a lover's waltz,
Shadows laugh as the daylight halts.

The moonlight's kiss on silken skin,
In the world of shadows, dreams begin.
Every glimmer, a story that grows,
Playing with light, where magic flows.

Under the stars, where secrets ignite,
Silhouettes dance in the depth of the night.
Echoes of laughter in a cosmic fight,
Shadows playing in the arms of light.

In the fading dusk, all is revealed,
Through gentle shadows, our fate is sealed.
Together they meet, the opposites unite,
In a timeless dance, shadows crave light.

Where Wishes Take Flight

In the night sky, stars gleam bright,
Whispers of dreams taking their flight.
Every hope, a flickering spark,
Guiding lost souls through the dark.

On the winds, sweet secrets soar,
Carried softly to distant shores.
Each promise woven in the breeze,
Awakens hearts, bringing them ease.

Through the clouds, the wishes weave,
Painting stories we believe.
With every heartbeat, they unfold,
A tapestry of dreams retold.

In the silence, a wish sets sail,
Bound for lands where hopes prevail.
Journeying far beyond our sight,
Into realms where wishes ignite.

Let your spirit rise and chase,
Find the dreams that time can't erase.
Together we'll create the night,
In the sky, where wishes take flight.

Fields of Illusion

Beneath the sky, a canvas wide,
Where shadows dance and dreams abide.
Golden fields in twilight's glow,
Murmuring tales only they know.

In the heart of the meadow's sway,
Whispers of magic softly play.
Every petal holds a sigh,
Enticing visions to drift by.

Illusions bloom like flowers rare,
Capturing visions beyond compare.
Each breeze carries stories untold,
As secrets unfold in hues bold.

Through the twilight, the colors blend,
Creating realms where dreams transcend.
In these fields, we lose our way,
Finding solace in the sway.

Here, reality takes a backseat,
As fantasies and lifetimes meet.
In fields of illusion, we roam free,
In a world where all dreams can be.

Dreams Dappled in Light

Softly falling, the moon's embrace,
Guiding dreams in a gentle space.
Each dappled form, a fleeting sight,
A dance of shadows in the night.

Golden beams on a silken stream,
Glow like whispers of a dream.
Every ripple, a tale unfurling,
Wrapped in warmth, fate twirling.

In the quiet, hopes ignite,
Painting hearts with pure delight.
With every breath, the magic swells,
Telling stories that time compels.

In this world, where spirits play,
Coloring moments that drift away.
Each specter of light, a wish we make,
Awakening dreams, for our souls' sake.

So linger softly in this enchant,
Where every chance finds room to plant.
In the glow of dreams, take flight,
In a realm forever bright.

The Dawn of Possibility

Morning light breaks the silent gray,
Chasing shadows of yesterday.
With every ray, new hopes arise,
Painting futures in sunny skies.

The world awakens, fresh and bright,
A canvas waiting for our light.
Each heartbeat a promise to keep,
In the dawn, our shadows leap.

Whispers of chance fill the air,
Inviting dreams beyond compare.
With open hearts, we dare to see,
All the wonders that can be.

Embracing change, we find our way,
Through the mist of a brand new day.
With courage, we step into the sun,
The dawn of possibility has begun.

So let the light guide your stride,
With every moment, dreams collide.
In this dawn, we rise and sing,
To the joys and hope that tomorrow brings.

Treasures in the Dusk

In twilight's glow the shadows play,
Whispers of secrets lost in gray.
Each moment holds a fleeting dream,
As time flows softly like a stream.

The stars emerge, a glimmering sight,
Guiding hearts through the veils of night.
In hidden paths, where hopes entwine,
We gather treasures, pure and fine.

The breeze carries tales from the past,
Of laughter shared that forever lasts.
Through every heartbeat, we discover,
In dusk's embrace, we find each other.

Footprints linger on the sandy shore,
Remnants of dreams that dare to soar.
With every sigh, the world feels new,
As dusk unfolds a vibrant hue.

So cherish these moments, fleeting yet bright,
In the tender arms of coming night.
For in the dusk, life's riches gleam,
As we weave our beautiful dream.

Beyond the Veil of Stars

Beyond the veil where starlight sings,
Cosmic wonders, grasping wings.
Each twinkle calls, a distant face,
Inviting us to join the chase.

Galaxies spin in a cosmic dance,
In the vastness, we take our chance.
With dreams ignited, hearts ablaze,
We reach for hope in a thousand ways.

Constellations draw the stories old,
Of heroes brave, and hearts of gold.
In whispers soft, the night reveals,
A tapestry of fate it seals.

We journey forth through endless space,
Finding solace in the embrace.
Each wish upon a shooting star,
Reminds us just how loved we are.

So let us wander, hand in hand,
Through cosmic realms, a boundless land.
For beyond the veil, our spirits soar,
Together facing forevermore.

Echoes of Aspirations

In quiet corners, whispers call,
Echoes of dreams that never fall.
Each heartbeat murmurs tales of hope,
A guiding light, a fragile rope.

Through valleys deep and mountains high,
We chase the clouds that fill the sky.
With every step, the pathway glows,
As our aspiration gently grows.

In shadows cast by fears we face,
We find the courage to embrace.
Through trials fierce, we carve our way,
With voices strong, a bright array.

The horizon beckons, wide and free,
A canvas broad, our legacy.
Each echo rings with truths we find,
As we unfold our joyful mind.

So lift your eyes to dreams anew,
With every dawn, the world feels true.
For in the echoes, we ignite,
A symphony of pure delight.

Canvases of the Infinite

On canvases, the colors blend,
In strokes of joy, our spirits mend.
Each paintbrush whispers tales untold,
Of passions deep, and hearts of gold.

In hues so bold, our visions soar,
An endless quest, forevermore.
With every line, our stories carve,
A masterpiece that none can starve.

From shades of blue to fiery red,
The dreams we weave, the words unsaid.
In every canvas, life unfolds,
A universe of wonders, bold.

Let inspiration guide the hand,
In visions bright, we take a stand.
A tapestry where hopes ignite,
In endless dance, we find our light.

So paint the world with colors bright,
In every shade, we find our light.
For in the canvas of the infinite,
Our souls reside, forever lit.

Arcadia of the Unseen

In the meadow, whispers flow,
Where dreams and shadows softly grow.
Hidden paths in the morning light,
Guide the hearts to take their flight.

Here, the unseen dances near,
Transforming worries into cheer.
Nature's canvas, rich and vast,
Echoes memories of the past.

Silence sings a melody sweet,
As sun and moon gently meet.
In every breeze, a story spun,
In this twilight, all is one.

An abode where spirits blend,
Where every journey finds its end.
Arcadia, where beauty gleams,
In the heart, we find our dreams.

Unseen wonders call our name,
In this realm, we're all aflame.
With every step, the world awakes,
In Arcadia, love never breaks.

Seeds of Inspiration

In the garden of fertile minds,
Grow the thoughts that fate unwinds.
Planting dreams like seeds in ground,
With the hope that they abound.

Each idea, a fragile start,
Waiting for a tender heart.
Watered with the light of day,
Nurtured in a gentle way.

See them sprout and reach for skies,
With colors bright, they mesmerize.
Branches stretch and flowers bloom,
Chasing off the shadows' gloom.

Inspiration's dance delights,
Illuminating starry nights.
With every whisper from the past,
New visions, wild and vast.

Harvest dreams when they are ripe,
Craft them into shades and type.
In the soil of our embrace,
Seeds of hope find their place.

Reveries in the Twilight

When the sun bows to the night,
Whispers wind with pure delight.
Stars awaken, softly gleam,
In the twilight's gentle dream.

Clouds like silk drift sweet and slow,
Painting skies in hues aglow.
Moments weave a tapestry,
Of fleeting time and mystery.

Softly echoes of the day,
In this hush they dance and play.
Lost in thoughts of yesteryears,
In the twilight, quiet fears.

Serenades on a sighing breeze,
Whispered secrets among the trees.
Memories linger, soft and light,
In reveries of fading light.

Each heartbeat marks a subtle pause,
In the silence, a cause to pause.
Embracing dusk with tender grace,
In twilight's warm, inviting space.

The Palette of New Beginnings

A canvas fresh, a world anew,
With colors bright, and skies of blue.
Brush in hand, the story starts,
As hope ignites within our hearts.

Each stroke whispers untold dreams,
In vibrant hues, the future beams.
Layers build like gentle waves,
In life's tide, the artist saves.

From charcoal grey to golden hues,
A symphony of vibrant views.
Each color speaks a tale profound,
In this palette, joy is found.

Moments captured, soft and bold,
In every shade, a tale unfolds.
The dawn awakes with tender light,
Painting shadows through the night.

Embrace the change in every stroke,
As life's canvas softly spoke.
In beginnings bright and clear,
The palette blooms, year after year.

Whispers of Tomorrow

In the quiet dawn, dreams arise,
Softly echoing through the skies.
Each whisper carries a gentle spark,
Guiding hearts through the unfolding dark.

Promises dance on the morning breeze,
Filling souls with a sense of ease.
Hope blooms bright where shadows fade,
Crafting paths where futures are laid.

Threads of fate in the fabric weave,
Beliefs uplifted, we dare to believe.
Tomorrow's light beams through the trees,
Enabling trust in life's mysteries.

As twilight falls, stars ignite,
Casting visions of the night.
A symphony of dreams to unfold,
Whispers of tomorrow, brave and bold.

With every breath, we seek and grow,
Carving images of what we know.
In the heart's embrace, we find our way,
Whispers leading to a brand new day.

Gardens of Ambition

In fields of green, ambitions thrive,
Watered by dreams, they come alive.
Each seed sown with care and trust,
Beneath the sun, they rise from dust.

Paths entwined with hopes anew,
Blossoms bright in every hue.
Through trials faced and fears tamed,
Our hearts are fierce, our spirits named.

With every storm, we bend but stand,
Nurtured by a steady hand.
In gardens rich, our goals take flight,
Reaching for the stars so bright.

As seasons change, we toil and reap,
Promises planted, memories deep.
Ambition fuels the fires we share,
Creating futures, bold and rare.

When the harvest comes, our dreams we find,
Blooming fiercely, intertwined.
In gardens of ambition, we will grow,
Together, the seeds of hope we sow.

Skylines of Hope

Beneath the stretch of evening's glow,
Skylines shimmer, dreams in tow.
Every building stands with grace,
A testament to hope's embrace.

In twilight's arms, we gather near,
Each heart a story, loud and clear.
With every pulse, a new refrain,
Carving strength from joy and pain.

Stars emerge as shadows blend,
In unity, our spirits mend.
Chasing visions, we dare to climb,
Scaling heights beyond all time.

With every step, horizons widen,
Through fractures of doubt, we confiden.
In the skyline's depths, our hopes ignite,
Bringing forth the dawn's first light.

Together, we'll rise, undeterred by night,
In the tapestry of dreams, we take flight.
Skylines standing tall, hearts entwined,
Echoing the hopes we seek to find.

Petals of Promise

Softly falling, petals drift,
In the garden where dreams uplift.
Colors vibrant, hues divine,
Each petal whispers, 'You are mine.'

Promises cradle in gentle hands,
Woven deep like ancient sands.
On breezes light, they dance and play,
Chasing shadows of yesterday.

In this space where futures bloom,
Hope arises, dispelling gloom.
Every fragrance tells a tale,
Of resilience found in love's veil.

With every petal, a wish is sown,
In the heart, connections grown.
Together we weave the paths we tread,
In the light where love is fed.

Petals of promise, soft and true,
Guide us forward in all we do.
In this garden where we belong,
Together we sing our hopeful song.

Dance of the Guiding Stars

In the dark where shadows play,
Stars awaken, bright and gay.
They twirl in a cosmic ballet,
Guiding souls who lose their way.

Whispers of the night unfold,
Dreams entwined in rays of gold.
Each spark a story to be told,
As the universe grows bold.

Winds of stardust softly blow,
Carrying tales from long ago.
They dance as if in secret show,
Illuminating paths below.

Galaxies in silence spin,
An endless waltz that won't grow thin.
Hearts awaken, drawn within,
The celestial dance begins.

Look up high, take in the sight,
Feel the wonder, pure delight.
In the dance of stars so bright,
Hope ignites the tranquil night.

Flowers Behind Closed Eyes

In the garden of the mind,
Flowers bloom, colors entwined.
Petals soft, their peace defined,
Hidden beauty, love enshrined.

Whispers of the fragrant breeze,
Stir the thoughts with gentle ease.
Each blossom brings its own reprise,
A symphony of heart's decrees.

Imagined blooms in radiant hues,
Crafting dreams, dissolving blues.
Silent echoes of morning dew,
In this world, the soul renews.

Behind closed eyes, reflections gleam,
In vibrant colors, visions teem.
A tranquil space, a waking dream,
Where reality and wonder beam.

Every petal holds a song,
Reminding us where we belong.
In this garden, love is strong,
Flourishing where hearts belong.

Pulses of Tomorrow's Land

In the earth, a heartbeat stirs,
Roots and dreams entwined in purrs.
Nature's pulse in whispered blurs,
Each moment a treasure that purrs.

Seeds of future bravely sown,
With every breath, new life is grown.
A canvas vast, unknown, alone,
Painting hopes with vibrant tone.

Skyward, visions start to rise,
With open hearts, we claim the skies.
Echoes of the past, a prize,
In unity, our strength lies.

Dreamers gather, hand in hand,
Building bridges 'cross the land.
Boundless futures, bright and grand,
In the warmth of hearts that stand.

With each step, we weave the thread,
Of the paths we long to tread.
For in our hearts, a flame is bred,
A hope that sails where dreams are led.

The Voyage of Secret Whispers

Upon the waves, the whispers glide,
Secrets dance with the ebbing tide.
Holding stories deep inside,
Where shadows and dreams collide.

Crafted tales in moonlit haze,
Guide the hearts through endless days.
In silence, hidden truths ablaze,
A journey forged in twilight's ways.

Fleeting moments, softly shared,
Carried forth when no one cared.
In the depths, where dreams are bared,
Hope resides, eternally paired.

Sailing forth on currents bold,
Every whisper, a tale retold.
With courage fierce, and love so gold,
We find our path, through mysteries hold.

Amidst the stars, we seek to find,
The secrets held in silence, kind.
For every heart, a map designed,
In the voyage, freedom aligned.

Sunrises of the Heart

Softly dawn begins to break,
Colors dance, the shadows wake.
Hope unfolds with gentle grace,
Sunlight kisses every face.

Whispers of a brand-new day,
Through the clouds, the light will play.
Each heartbeat, a promise true,
In the warmth, I rise anew.

Golden rays on velvet skies,
Lifting dreams that dare to rise.
In the stillness, love ignites,
Filling hearts with pure delights.

Echoes of the night are gone,
In the light, our spirits drawn.
Sunrises bloom, a sacred art,
Painting joy upon the heart.

Chasing the Candle's Flame

In the dark, a flicker glows,
A tiny light that gently flows.
Guiding paths through shadow's night,
Chasing dreams that feel so right.

Hands outstretched, we reach our goal,
The candle's fire warms the soul.
Flickering hopes in whispered air,
We chase the glow, a dance so rare.

Burning bright, the struggles fade,
In the light, our fears evade.
With each step, we draw so near,
To the warmth that conquers fear.

Embers spark through dusky gloom,
Creating joy, dispelling doom.
In the chase, we find our peace,
Chasing flames that never cease.

Through the night, we carry dreams,
In the candle's light, it seems.
Together, bright, we will remain,
Chasing hope, like candle's flame.

Fables Woven in Air

In the breeze, stories unfold,
Whispers of legends, bright and bold.
Woven tales in the sky so high,
Each soft cloud, a lullaby.

Tales of heroes, lost and found,
Echoes of laughter, joy resound.
Through the ages, they will flow,
Fables shared with hearts aglow.

Secrets carried on the wind,
With each gust, new dreams begin.
In the rustle of each leaf,
Find the magic, share belief.

Mountains rise and rivers bend,
Nature's stories never end.
Through the air, we learn and grow,
Fables in currents, soft and slow.

As we listen, worlds invite,
In the air, there's pure delight.
Fables woven, hearts embrace,
In the sky, we find our place.

Meadows of the Mind

In the meadows of our thought,
Dreams and visions gently caught.
Fields of blue and blades of green,
Where the mind can dance and glean.

Winds of change rustle the grass,
Thoughts that wander, moments pass.
In the quiet, clarity blooms,
Filling hearts with bright perfumes.

Sunset brings a golden hue,
Painting skies, a canvas true.
In the twilight, we reflect,
On the beauty we detect.

Pathways weave through every space,
In this meadow, find your place.
Freedom dances in the air,
In the mind, we find our care.

Cherished moments, like a song,
In these meadows, we belong.
Thoughts will flourish, hearts entwined,
In the peace of the mind's meadows.

Petals of Promise in the Wind

Petals drift softly, like whispered dreams,
Carried by breezes, bursting with themes.
They dance in the sunlight, a twinkling flight,
Embracing the stories of day and night.

Each fold tells a tale, of joy and of pain,
Of love that was lost, and bonds that remain.
In gardens of hope, the colors ignite,
A mosaic of wishes, so brilliant, so bright.

The wind carries secrets, both old and anew,
As whispers of nature weave through the view.
With each gentle flutter, a promise revealed,
In the heart of the moment, true magic is healed.

Nature's soft symphony, played on a loop,
Calls forth our spirits to gather and stoop.
To gather the petals, and cherish each one,
In the dance of existence, life's thread has been spun.

So let us rejoice in the waves of the air,
For petals of promise are floating out there.
Each moment in time, let us hold and defend,
As we weave the fabric of love without end.

Echoes of Aspirations Unfurled

In the quiet dawn, dreams begin to rise,
Whispered ambitions, reaching for skies.
Each echo resounds, with fervor and grace,
As hearts open wide, to embrace their place.

Moments of courage, they beckon and call,
To seize every chance, to rise and not fall.
With clarity gained, we step to the beat,
Unraveling visions, making life sweet.

Through valleys of doubt, through mountains of fear,
Aspirations soar, growing ever clear.
With voices united, our hopes intertwine,
Creating a tapestry, brilliantly fine.

Each path that we choose, while daunting, is bright,
Illuminated pathways, leading to light.
In shadows we find, the strength to be bold,
With echoes of dreams, our stories unfold.

So let us ignite the fire within,
For aspirations linger, both fragile and thin.
Through trials and triumphs, we'll rise, undeterred,
In the symphony of life, our voices are heard.

Landscapes of the Heart Awakening

Awake to the dawn, where the wildflowers bloom,
In landscapes of dreams, dispelling the gloom.
Each petal, a heartbeat, each breeze, a sigh,
Awakening passions that reach for the sky.

The rivers of hope, they carve through the stone,
Flowing with purpose, they journey alone.
In valleys of silence, beneath canopies wide,
The heart finds its rhythm, no longer to hide.

Mountains rise tall, with their wisdom to lend,
Guardians of secrets, where footsteps transcend.
With each gentle whisper, the soul starts to soar,
In landscapes of longing, we seek evermore.

Sunsets paint stories, in colors so bold,
The canvas of life, in hues manifold.
As shadows retreat, and the night starts to gleam,
New landscapes emerge, igniting each dream.

In the tapestry woven from moments so dear,
The heart awakens, dissolving all fear.
With each breath we take, let us nurture this ground,
In landscapes of love, true freedom is found.

The Palette of Infinite Possibilities

Open the box, let the colors ignite,
With strokes of the future, dreams taking flight.
Each hue, a potential, an endless array,
Inviting the heart to discover the way.

Brushes of moments, held tender and tight,
Create a collage, transform dark into light.
In swirls of imagination, passion does spill,
In the palette of life, we craft our own will.

A splash of pure joy, a dash of deep pain,
Each color a story, of loss and of gain.
Layer upon layer, the canvas expands,
With every decision, we shape our own hands.

Infinite options, like stars in the night,
Sparkling with wonder, guiding our sight.
In the mix of perception, we dance and we weave,
The palette of possibilities, all we believe.

So paint with abandon, let your spirit flow,
For the masterpiece crafted will endlessly grow.
In the light of creation, may we always find peace,
In the palette of life, our passions release.

Kaleidoscope of Possibilities

Colors swirl and blend anew,
Every turn reveals a view.
Shapes that dance within the light,
Endless paths in day and night.

Dreams ignite and shimmer bright,
Whispers of a future's flight.
In this glass, we find our way,
Chasing visions, come what may.

Each reflection paints a tale,
Where belief cannot grow stale.
Fractals of what could have been,
A tapestry of hopes unseen.

From the mundane, magic calls,
Every flicker, wonder sprawls.
In this journey, hearts entwine,
Creating worlds in every line.

So embrace the vibrant hue,
Let your spirit start anew.
In the chaos, find the grace,
Kaleidoscopes, our dreams embrace.

The Eye of the Dreamer

In the hush where visions dwell,
The dreamer spins a magic spell.
With eyes wide open, hearts align,
Crafting realms both rare and fine.

Winds of change begin to blow,
Carrying thoughts where few dare go.
An artist's heart, a canvas bare,
Painting hopes in vibrant air.

Through shadows deep, a light breaks free,
Unraveling dreams like waves at sea.
With every heartbeat, stories rise,
In the quiet, truth belies.

A flicker here, a whisper there,
The dreamer breathes in endless air.
Harvesting stars from midnight's weave,
In the silence, we believe.

So linger near the silver skies,
Where the eye of magic lies.
In dreams, the world expands and bends,
As the dreamer softly mends.

Fountains of Infinite Thoughts

Beneath the surface, whispers flow,
Fountains where the mind can grow.
From depths unseen, ideas sprout,
Waves of wonder twist about.

In each droplet, stories gleam,
Cascades of light, a waking dream.
Sculpting visions, pure and clear,
Voices echo, drawing near.

Thoughts like rivers, winding, free,
In every turn, a mystery.
With each splash, a journey starts,
A dance of minds and tender hearts.

So dip your hand in waters true,
Let inspiration come to you.
Fountains burst with wisdom's grace,
In every drop, a sacred space.

For in the flow of endless streams,
Lie the seeds of cherished dreams.
With each thought, a world takes flight,
Fountains sparkle in the night.

Journeys Yet to Be Told

Every step upon the ground,
Holds the stories yet unbound.
With each breath, a tale begins,
Where the heart's quiet yearning spins.

Maps unseen, horizons vast,
Whispers of the future cast.
Through the valleys, over hills,
Time unfolds with gentle thrills.

Paths uncertain, courage sings,
In the midst of all life brings.
Every moment, sharp and bright,
Guides our journeys toward the light.

With the dawn, a promise wakes,
Every choice the soul remakes.
In the stillness, dreams ignite,
Venturing forth, spirits take flight.

So wander wild, embrace the roam,
For every traveler finds a home.
Journeys whisper, stories swell,
In the heart, all will be well.

Beyond the Veil of Ordinary

In whispers soft, the secrets dwell,
Where dreams unfold, and stories swell.
A world unseen, a hidden gain,
Beyond the veil, the life's refrain.

Beneath the stars, time takes its flight,
Through realms of magic, pure delight.
Each step we take, a thread unwinds,
In depths unknown, the heart still finds.

The ordinary fades, the magic calls,
As shadows dance on ancient walls.
In every breath, the wonder stays,
In every glance, the spirit plays.

A tapestry of moments spun,
Where hearts collide, and souls are one.
Beyond the veil, we dare to soar,
To touch the dreams we can't ignore.

So journey forth, embrace the light,
In every shadow, find your sight.
For in the dance of calm and storm,
Beyond the veil, our hearts transform.

Skylines Painted with Ambitions

Each dawn brings forth a canvas bright,
With strokes of dreams, we chase the light.
Buildings rise, like hopes on high,
In every corner, futures lie.

With every step, we carve our names,
In bustling streets and city games.
Ambitions flow like rivers wide,
Building bridges, breaking tide.

The skyline glows with endless schemes,
A patchwork quilt of fervent dreams.
The hustle echoes, hearts aligned,
In every challenge, courage finds.

Colors clash in vibrant ways,
As aspirations shape our days.
With every heart, a story sparks,
In shadows cast, igniting arcs.

So let us rise, with spirits bold,
To paint our tales in strokes of gold.
For every skyline holds the key,
To worlds of wonder, yet to be.

A Symphony of Future Echoes

In quiet moments, whispers play,
A symphony of dreams today.
Each note a step towards the dawn,
In echoes soft, our fears are gone.

The future hums a tune unknown,
In every heart, a seed is sown.
With visions bright, we start to sing,
In harmony, the futures bring.

With every choice, a melody,
Creating paths for you and me.
Through trials faced, we find our sound,
In every loss, new hope is found.

Resonance builds, a vibrant thread,
Connecting all, where none are led.
The symphony of life unfolds,
In each heartbeat, the future holds.

So join the dance, embrace the flow,
Together, let our visions grow.
For in this song, our spirits soar,
A journey shared, forevermore.

The Dance of Light and Shadow

In twilight's glow, the shadows weave,
A dance of light, where dreams believe.
Each flicker tells a tale so clear,
In moments grasped, we draw them near.

With every step, the contrasts play,
In shades of dusk, we find our way.
Where light embraces, shadows blend,
A tapestry that never ends.

The rhythm of the night unfolds,
In whispered secrets, stories told.
With each heartbeat, we find the grace,
In every glance, a soft embrace.

Through alleys dark and paths of bright,
We dance between the day and night.
For every shadow holds a spark,
Illuminating what is dark.

So let us twirl in life's grand show,
Where light and shadow ebb and flow.
For in this dance, we deeply find,
A union forged, forever twined.

Awakening the Nightingale

In twilight's gentle cradle, she sings,
A melody of dreams on silver wings.
The stars alight with whispers, soft and bright,
As shadows dance, embracing the night.

Beneath the moon's embrace, a tender hush,
Where secrets stir and sleepy hearts rush.
Her song ignites the fire in the dark,
A symphony of life, igniting the spark.

With each note, petals fall from above,
Awakening the world to a language of love.
In stillness, the heart begins to play,
As the nightingale calls, leading the way.

The dawn will greet her with a gentle sigh,
Yet for now, beneath stars, she will fly.
In every shadow, her voice will remain,
A testament to peace, joy, and pain.

So listen close, to the nightingale's plight,
In her song is the heart of the night.
With courage and grace, she'll find her flight,
Awakening dreams under soft moonlight.

Veils of Untold Mysteries

In twilight's weave, the secrets remain,
Each thread a whisper of joy and pain.
Veils obscure the truth within,
A dance of shadows where stories begin.

The forest breathes, a thousand tales spun,
In rustling leaves, the forgotten run.
Beneath the surface, the silence weaves,
Stories of hearts and the dreams that it leaves.

Eyes gazing deep into the hidden lore,
Every glance a key to an open door.
Mysteries echo through the hollow trees,
With the wind as witness, carried on the breeze.

The moonlit path, a guide through the night,
Illuminating wisdom obscured from sight.
With each soft step, the journey unfolds,
Veils lifted gently, revealing bold.

In the quiet whispers of dusk now clear,
Life's untold tales draw ever near.
Embrace the unknown, let curiosity reign,
In depths of silence, the heart will sustain.

Trellises of Bravery

Beneath the weight of fears we stand tall,
In gardens of courage, we will not fall.
Each vine a testament of will and fight,
Reaching for dreams, stretching toward the light.

With every struggle, a flower will bloom,
In the face of doubt, dispelling the gloom.
Nature's embrace, a structure so strong,
Lifting our spirits, guiding us along.

Weaving our hopes through moments of pain,
Finding our solace in sunlight and rain.
The trellises speak of journeys so grand,
Where bravery flourishes, hand in hand.

Buds of defiance in the fiercest storm,
Love and resilience, a sheltering form.
As seasons change, our roots dig in deep,
In the face of a storm, our promise we keep.

So climb, dear heart, to the heights you deserve,
In the trellises of bravery, find your nerve.
Nurtured by hope, we rise from the ground,
With every heartbeat, our dreams will resound.

Familiar Strangers on the Path

Amid the crowd, I see a kindred face,
Our paths entwined in this busy place.
Familiar yet unknown, we share a glance,
In silent understanding, we take the chance.

With each step forward, time begins to blur,
Whispers of stories in every soft stir.
Moments fleeting, like shadows at play,
Familiar strangers glide along the way.

The laughter shared amidst the mundane,
Threads of connection, joy and pain.
Together we wander through life's vast page,
In twinkling eyes, we find the sage.

Each heartbeat echoes a rhythm profound,
In the dance of strangers, we're ever bound.
With every turn, new stories unfold,
In the tapestry of life, rich and bold.

So let us embrace this journey anew,
As familiar strangers, with hearts so true.
In every moment, shared laughter and sighs,
We'll cherish the journey, where connection lies.

Whispers of Dawn's Embrace

Softly the light begins to creep,
Gentle whispers where shadows sleep.
With every breeze, hope starts to rise,
Painting dreams across the skies.

Awakening petals, stretch and sway,
In this moment, night drifts away.
Birds take flight, their songs so sweet,
A new day dawns where hearts may meet.

Golden rays through leaves do filter,
The chill of night begins to a smilter.
Rustling branches echo the day,
As life unfolds in vibrant array.

Time unfolds like petals in bloom,
Casting away all shadows of gloom.
In the hush, a promise takes form,
Embracing all in love's warm.

With each heartbeat, the world feels anew,
A tender canvas in gentle hues.
Embrace the whispers, feel the grace,
In the dawn's soft, warm embrace.

Gardens of Tomorrow's Light

In gardens where dreams intertwine,
Future blooms in the sun's warm shine.
Tethered hopes in roots take hold,
Visions painted in hues so bold.

Each seed sown tells a tale untold,
Of courage and love, fierce and bold.
Whispers of fate on the soft, warm breeze,
Unfolding wonders beneath the trees.

Petals unfurl with the morning dew,
A dance of color, a vibrant hue.
Promises linger in the fragrant air,
As nature weaves magic with utmost care.

Time drips slow like honeyed gold,
Secrets of life in their beauty unfold.
With every sunrise, a new start,
Gardens of tomorrow, held in the heart.

So tend to the blooms, nurture each dream,
Let your spirit and passion gleam.
In these gardens, let love take flight,
Awakening souls to tomorrow's light.

The Canvas of Unwritten Skies

Overhead looms a canvas vast,
With colors of dreams from ages past.
Brushstrokes of clouds, soft and free,
Whispers of what is yet to be.

The wind carries tales on its breath,
Stories of life, of love, of death.
Each star a wish waiting to shine,
In the depths of the heavens divine.

When twilight falls, shadows convene,
Dancing lightly in shades of green.
A tapestry woven with silken threads,
Night's embrace where magic spreads.

Hope glimmers softly in the dark,
A gentle flicker, a warming spark.
Though unwritten, the lines will flow,
With every heartbeat, letting dreams grow.

So gaze upon these skies of that bloom,
A canvas of promise that harbors no gloom.
For every dawn paints anew the lore,
In the pages of life, waiting to explore.

Where Stars Align in Secret

In the quiet night, whispers entwine,
Where secrets are held, and souls align.
Stars twinkle softly in velvet skies,
Guiding lost hearts with ancient ties.

Mysteries whisper through moonlit beams,
Unraveling tales born from our dreams.
Each constellation telling its lore,
Of love and longing, forevermore.

Underneath this blanket of night,
Hearts discover their hidden light.
Connection found in the silence deep,
Promises made, we dare to keep.

Every gaze cast toward the above,
In the dance of starlight, we find our love.
Fates intertwine like threads of gold,
Stories of passion and hearts so bold.

In the stillness, the cosmos unfolds,
A map of dreams and tales retold.
Where stars align, so do we dare,
In the magic of night, we lay our care.

Seeds of Stardust in the Mind's Eye

In the depths where dreams reside,
Whispers of the cosmos glide.
Each thought a spark, a glowing stream,
Sowing seeds of a brilliant dream.

Nebulas swirl in silence deep,
Cradled in the mind's soft sweep.
Visions dance like stars at night,
Guiding lost souls to the light.

Flickering flames of endless grace,
Unfolding warmth in a vast space.
Harvesting thoughts, a radiant flight,
Chasing shadows, embracing light.

In each moment, a galaxy spins,
Cascading wonders, where life begins.
A universe crafted from purest sighs,
Mapping journeys beneath the skies.

With each heartbeat, the cosmos sings,
Authored by dreams, the joy it brings.
In stardust whispers, the mind expands,
Painting colors with gentle hands.

Awakening the Colors of Hope

Amidst the gray, a hint of hue,
Dancing shades break through the blue.
Promises linger in the air,
Awakening dreams, a vibrant flair.

Gentle winds whisper soft and clear,
Carrying wishes for all to hear.
Each petal blooms, a tale anew,
Colors of hope, forever true.

Emerald greens and golden rays,
Paint the canvas of brighter days.
In every heartbeat, a pulse of light,
Guiding us through the darkest night.

From ashes rise the flames of change,
Transforming hearts in a world so strange.
Awakening spirits, bold and bright,
Chasing shadows to claim the light.

With every dawn, the colors sing,
Life reawakens, fresh and spring.
Hope ignites beneath the skies,
A symphony of endless highs.

A Tapestry Woven with Wishes

Threads of desire in colors unite,
Crafting dreams with shimmering light.
A tapestry woven, both bold and fine,
Each stitch a heartbeat, a fragile line.

Along the loom of time we weave,
Patterns of joy, we dare to believe.
With hands of love, we pull and spin,
Creating a world where dreams begin.

Every wish a thread, a story to tell,
Binding our hearts in a magical spell.
Hope intertwines with the fabric of fate,
A dance of creation, where dreams await.

In hues of laughter, sorrows release,
Spiraling stories, stitched with peace.
The woven dreams shall never fray,
As we embrace each passing day.

With every turn, the colors bloom,
Erasing shadows, dispelling gloom.
A tapestry crafted, forever we share,
In the warmth of wishes, we find our care.

The Breath of New Beginnings

In the silence of dawn's first light,
Awakens whispers, pure and bright.
A gentle breeze, a tender sigh,
Bringing forth the chance to fly.

With each heartbeat, the world ignites,
Embracing change on diamond nights.
The breath of hope fills the air,
Inviting dreams with loving care.

Old chapters close, new ones unfold,
Stories waiting to be told.
With open hearts, we glide and sway,
Sowing seeds for a brighter day.

Through trials faced, we learn to rise,
Finding strength in every surprise.
The dawn breaks forth, a canvas wide,
Illuminating paths where love resides.

A symphony echoes, fresh and true,
The breath of beginnings starts anew.
With each moment, we are free,
Embracing life's sweet reverie.

Flickers of Celestial Dreams

Stars whisper softly, in the night sky,
Wishing on dreams that twinkle nearby.
The moon casts shadows, a silver glow,
Guiding lost souls where night rivers flow.

Comets blaze trails, through the velvet dark,
Echoes of wishes, igniting a spark.
Galaxies spin, in a cosmic dance,
Holding our hopes in a timeless trance.

Nebulas swirl, in colors so bright,
Painting the canvas of dreams in flight.
Each flicker of light, a story untold,
Whispers of futures, both brave and bold.

In the vast silence, we find our dreams,
Floating like feathers on moonlit beams.
A tapestry woven of heart and night,
Flickers of wishes, a wondrous sight.

The heavens above, our spirits align,
In this celestial realm, our fates intertwine.
Embrace the magic, let your heart soar,
With flickers of dreams, we forever explore.

Twilight's Embrace

As day bids farewell, the shadows creep,
In twilight's embrace, the world falls asleep.
Colors blend softly, as dusk takes its place,
A blanket of stars, a warm, gentle space.

Whispers of breezes, secrets they share,
Caressing the night, like a lover's care.
Moonlight cascades, through branches and leaves,
Painting the path for those who believe.

Fireflies dance, in the cool evening air,
Guiding us softly, to places so rare.
With every heartbeat, the night starts to sing,
Melodies woven, in dreams we will bring.

The horizon shimmers, where shadows reside,
In twilight's embrace, all worries subside.
A haven of peace, a moment divine,
Wrapped in the stillness, our spirits entwine.

Let the dusk hold you, in its gentle fold,
A story unfolding, in whispers of old.
Twilight, a promise, of dreams yet to chase,
In the quiet of night, we find our own grace.

Dreams Encircling the Dawn

When night pulls away, revealing the glow,
Dreams encircle dawn, in a tender show.
Sunrise ignites, with colors ablaze,
Chasing the shadows, through misty haze.

Birds take to flight, in a chorus of cheer,
Welcoming daylight, as morning draws near.
The world awakens, from slumbering sighs,
With hopes and with wishes, that touch the skies.

Each ray of sunlight, a promise, a song,
Reminding us softly, where we all belong.
Dreams intertwining, with the thrill of the day,
Unfolding like petals, in bright, golden sway.

Embrace the new light, as shadows retreat,
In the dance of the dawn, feel your heart beat.
The canvas of morning, brushed wide and free,
Paints visions of life, where our spirits will be.

In this sacred moment, as night takes a bow,
Dreams encircling dawn, whispering now.
Step boldly into what the day has in store,
For dreams are the key, to unlock every door.

The Language of Skylines

In the hush of the twilight glow,
Buildings rise, wordless and slow.
Their shadows stretch, stories weave,
Echoes of dreams that we believe.

Each rooftop whispers ancient tales,
Of love and loss, of ships and sails.
Glass reflects the colors of night,
A canvas painted with sheer delight.

Beneath the stars, the city breathes,
A pulse of life, in whispers wreathed.
Its heartbeat syncs with hopes and fears,
In quiet corners, laughter cheers.

The skyline speaks to those who see,
A language vast, wild, and free.
In every silhouette, a wish,
A fragile chance, a fleeting bliss.

Together we rise, hand in hand,
Building dreams upon this land.
In the skyline's grasp, we find our way,
A promise of dawn in shades of gray.

Epiphanies of the Dawn

Morning breaks with gentle grace,
A soft touch on nature's face.
Birds take flight, the world awakes,
In every heart, a new hope makes.

Golden rays kiss the waking earth,
Heralding dreams of rebirth.
Shadows flee, in colors bold,
Stories waiting to be told.

Glistening dew on the grass does gleam,
Each drop a part of a waking dream.
Life emerges, vibrant and bright,
An epiphany, a delight.

In the hush of the morning's breath,
Resilience blooms, defying death.
With every ray, a chance to grow,
Awakening hearts to the glow.

As the sun climbs high in the sky,
We lift our voices, let them fly.
With gratitude, we embrace the dawn,
Epiphanies of hope reborn.

Threads of Unseen Futures

In the silence of the night,
Stars weave tales, pure and bright.
Threads of fate, in shadows spun,
Dreams entangle, one by one.

With every breath, we cast our hopes,
Winding paths, like silk, elopes.
In the tapestry of what may be,
Possibilities weave endlessly.

Fingers trace the fabric's glow,
Mysteries hidden, deep below.
Yet in the heart, a compass lies,
Guiding us through starlit skies.

Each choice a stitch, each tear a chance,
Reweaving life in a dance.
Embracing change as time unfolds,
Future's story waits to be told.

Threads of unseen futures bind,
A world of wonder we must find.
While the universe dances wide,
In our hearts, the dreams abide.

Elysium in the Making

In gardens lush, where whispers sing,
Hope takes root, a vibrant spring.
Petals soft, the colors blend,
Nature's canvas, without end.

Every heartbeat feels the art,
An Elysium born from the heart.
With every seed, a dream is sown,
In fertile ground, we find our home.

With sunlit skies and moonlit nights,
We chase the shadows, seek the lights.
In unity, we rise as one,
Beneath the glow of the golden sun.

In laughter shared, in kindness shown,
Together, we make the unknown.
With hands entwined, we'll build the way,
To Elysium, come what may.

Each moment cherished, every sigh,
A step closer to the sky.
In this journey, dreams we stake,
An Elysium in the making.

Chasing the Sunlit Pathways

Beneath the wide and azure sky,
We tread on trails where shadows lie.
Footsteps dance on golden light,
In whispers soft, the day turns bright.

Through meadows lush and forests deep,
Awake the dreams that we shall keep.
With every turn, the heart takes flight,
Chasing the sun, our souls ignite.

The breeze carries laughter's call,
With painted skies, we rise, we fall.
On pathways rich with nature's art,
Together we shall never part.

The journey winds, yet we are bold,
Each moment savored, stories told.
With every step, the world unfolds,
A tapestry in fiery gold.

In twilight's glow, our spirits play,
The sunlit pathways guide our way.
With open hearts and hands held tight,
We'll dance into the night's delight.

Nature's Call to Dreamers

In the hush of dawn, dreams arise,
Nature beckons with gentle sighs.
Birdsongs weave through branches high,
While petals open to the sky.

Soft rustles call the wandering hearts,
In quiet woods where magic starts.
A symphony of colors blend,
In every leaf, a tale to send.

Beneath the stars, our wishes soar,
In nature's arms, we find the core.
With every breeze, inspirations flow,
A fertile ground for dreams to grow.

Mountains stand tall like ancient dreams,
Reflecting life in silvery streams.
Together we chase the rising sun,
Nature's call, forever spun.

In meadows lush, we lay and gaze,
While time slips softly, lost in haze.
Dreamers of both heart and mind,
In nature's cradle, peace we find.

The Light Beyond the Fog

A shroud of mist hangs in the air,
Whispers of secrets, dreams laid bare.
Yet somewhere beyond the dim embrace,
A spark of light begins to chase.

Footsteps echo on dampened ground,
In silence soft, new hope is found.
Each breath adorned with morning dew,
The light ahead sharpens our view.

The fog may linger, but so shall we,
In pursuit of what's meant to be.
With hearts aglow, we lean into,
The warmth that guides our journey true.

Each ray unfolds like stories old,
Of dreams deferred, yet still so bold.
As shadows fade, our spirits rise,
Finding our path beneath the skies.

With every step, the fog unwinds,
Revealing treasures that fate finds.
Together we'll walk, hand in hand,
Towards the light, a promised land.

Blooming Beyond the Boundaries

In hidden corners where shadows dwell,
A flower blooms; it knows too well.
Against the odds, it stretches wide,
With colors bright, it cannot hide.

Breaking free from the earth's tight clutch,
With roots that hold and petals such.
Each bud a promise, fierce and bold,
A testament to stories told.

Through rocky paths and muted tones,
Life dares to thrive, in fields it owns.
With every thorn, it bears its crown,
A beauty forged that won't back down.

Beyond the fences of doubt's design,
A garden blooms, distinct and fine.
Each bloom declares, with vibrant grace,
"No boundary holds this sacred space."

As seasons shift and colors wane,
The spirit of growth will ever reign.
From every tear, new strength expands,
Blooming wild in freedom's hands.

Ripples of Unwritten Stories

In the quiet of the night, they call,
Whispers dancing softly, a gentle thrall.
Each echo, a heartbeat, a tale left untold,
Ripples of dreams in the waters of old.

Winds weave through shadows, secrets in flight,
Unraveled in moments, lost to the light.
Yet still they linger, like stars in the dark,
Ripples of stories, igniting a spark.

In the rustle of leaves, the stories unfold,
Silent yet vibrant, inscribed in the bold.
Each shadow a journey, each pause a refrain,
Ripples of wonder, joy mingled with pain.

Through time and through space, they weave and they
flow,
Like rivers of thoughts that steadily grow.
Each voice is a tremor, each sigh is a thread,
Ripples of tales from the heart and the head.

So listen, dear traveler, to what lies beneath,
The ripples of stories that life hath bequeathed.
For every adventure, a marker will stay,
Ripples of unwritten, guiding the way.

Lightscapes of the Imagination

In the realm of dreams, where visions ignite,
Colors cascade in the depths of the night.
Beneath the still surface, new worlds start to gleam,
Lightscapes unfolding, a magical dream.

Brush strokes of thought paint the skies,
Sparkles of wonder, like stars, they arise.
Imaginations flutter, taking their flight,
Lightscapes surrounding, dazzling the sight.

In whispers of twilight, ideas take form,
A tapestry woven, vibrant and warm.
Each flicker a journey, each shimmer a song,
Lightscapes of freedom where hearts truly belong.

Through corridors vast, let your spirit roam,
In gardens of colors, let your mind build a home.
With each gentle whisper, new visions will bloom,
Lightscapes of the heart, dispelling the gloom.

So dream with abandon, let your soul take flight,
In the lightscapes of wonder, embrace the delight.
For here in the glow, your essence will shine,
Lightscapes of imagination, forever divine.

Secrets Carried by the Wind

Secrets swirl gently, the breeze softly sighs,
Echoes of whispers brushed past the skies.
Each rustle a tale of what once came to be,
Secrets carried by the wind, wild and free.

Through valleys and mountains, they wander and weave,
A dance with the twilight, a night to believe.
In hushed tones they murmur, in currents they flow,
Secrets of ages, both tender and slow.

From flowers that bloom to the falcon's keen call,
These truths of the world find a home in us all.
With every soft gust, a new story's unfurled,
Secrets in motion, connecting the world.

So listen, dear traveler, to whispers around,
In the tales of the wind, life's essence is found.
For every soft breech is a chance to ascend,
Secrets carried by the wind, they never end.

In the silence of moments, in laughter and cries,
The wind holds our secrets, the truth never lies.
With open hearts journey, let freedom unfold,
Secrets carried by the wind, worth more than gold.

Blossoms of Tomorrow

In the dawn of a dream, new petals will bloom,
Whispers of promise dispel the cold gloom.
Each moment a miracle waiting to show,
Blossoms of tomorrow, budding to grow.

With courage like sunlight, they break through the night,
Filling the world with enchanting delight.
Fragile but strong, they dance in the air,
Blossoms of tomorrow, a vision so rare.

Through gardens of hope, let your spirit take flight,
In vibrant abundance, embrace the soft light.
Each bloom tells a story, each fragrance a song,
Blossoms of tomorrow where hearts are made strong.

So gather the courage to reach for the sky,
In the dance of the blossoms, let your dreams fly.
For every new flower ignites the soul's flame,
Blossoms of tomorrow, forever the same.

With time as the gardener, let patience unfold,
The beauty of blossoms, a tale to be told.
In fields of abundance, let love always flow,
Blossoms of tomorrow, in hearts we will sow.

www.ingramcontent.com/pod-product-compliance
Ingram Content Group UK Ltd.
Pitfield, Milton Keynes, MK11 3LW, UK
UKHW031611161224
3696UKWH00040B/530